SIGHT WORD FLUENCY READING

FIVE Languages

Improve Your Child's Reading Skills

English German French Spanish - Chinese

Box   boîte

box

caja   框

The box is full of clothes.

Bär   ours

bear

oso   熊

The bear likes to eat honey.

Fenster   fenêtre

window

ventana   窗口

The window is open.

Bein — jambe

leg

pierna — 腿

My leg is feeling better.

Füße — pieds

feet

pies — 脚

His feet are swollen.

Beispiel — exemple

example

ejemplo — 例

This is an example of a bird.

Baum   arbre

tree

árbol   树

She is sitting under a tree.

Kuchen   gâteau

cake

pastel   蛋糕

The cake is white and pink.

Ergebnis   but

score

puntuación   得分了

What was the final score?

Geburtstag

anniversaire

birthday

cumpleaños

生日

Today is my birthday.

Apfel

pomme

apple

manzana

苹果

Apples are a popular fruit.

Regen

pluie

rain

lluvia

雨

We love the rain!

Vogel

oiseau

bird

pájaro

鸟

The bird is dancing happily.

Idee

idée

idea

idea

理念

I have an idea!

Katze

chat

cat

gato

猫

That cat is adorable.

Wind — vent

wind

viento — 风

The wind blows the leaves.

Spielzeug — jouet

toy

juguete — 玩具

He has a whole box of toys.

Büro — bureau

office

oficina — 办公室

Do you need any office supplies?

Garten

jardin

garden

jardín

花园

They are going to the garden.

Feuer

feu

fire

fuego

火

Fire is hot.

Tür

porte

door

puerta

门

He is knocking on the door.

Mädchen   fille

girl

niña   女孩

The girl is pretty.

Farmer   fermier

farmer

agricultor   农民

The farmer had a farm.

Kitty   minou

kitty

gatito   猫咪

I like my kitty.

Boden   sol

ground

suelo   地面

It plays a trick on the ground.

Essen   aliments

food

comida   餐饮

They made a lot of food.

Schule   école

school

colegio   学校

They are going to school.

Seite — page

page

página — 页

Please turn the page.

Lied — chanson

song

canciones — 歌曲

She is singing a song.

Tag — journée

day

día — 天

This day is the 30th.

Holz / bois

wood

madera / 木

He plays with wooden blocks

Glocke / cloche

bell

campana / 钟

I hear the bell ringing!

Fußboden / sol

floor

suelo / 地板

The girl sits on the floor.

Milch   lait

milk

leche   牛奶

The baby is drinking milk.

Kinder   les enfants

children

niños   孩子们

Four children sang.

Bett   lit

bed

cama   床

We all share three beds.

Hase

lapin

rabbit

conejo

兔子

The rabbit wants to play.

Hund

chien

dog

perro

狗

The dog wants to eat sweets.

Kopf

tête

head

cabeza

头

She has a hat on her head.

time

He is telling the time.

cotton

A q-tip is made of cotton.

robin

The robin is helping Santa.

Stock   bâton

stick

palo   棒

He is playing sticks.

Mantel   manteau

coat

saco   涂层

She is wearing her coat.

---

vier   quatre

four

cuatro   四

There were four of them.

Hügel   colline

hill

colina   爬坡道

The house is on the hill.

Nest   nid

nest

nido   巢

The bird has a nest.

Wasser   l'eau

water

agua   水

He is drinking water.

sister

She is my sister.

sheep

The sheep have fluffy wool.

game

What game is it?

Hähnchen   poulet

chicken

pollo   小鸡

The chicken is laying eggs.

Ort   endroit

place

sitio   地点

This is my favorite place.

Gesicht   visage

face

cara   面对

They were at the face painting booth.

Kinder

les enfants

children

niños

孩子们

The children are playing.

Mann

homme

man

hombre

男子

This man is my dad.

Bruder

frère

brother

hermano

哥哥

They are brothers.

Party

party

fiesta

fête

派对

I love to go to parties.

Schuh

shoe

zapato

chaussure

鞋

I have new shoes.

Brot

bread

un pan

pain

面包

She is baking some bread.

Hand
main
hand
mano
手
You should wash your hands.

Papier
papier
paper
papel
纸
I like to color on paper.

Name
nom
name
nombre
名称
My name is Joe.

Joe

Zuhause

maison

home

casa

家

He drew a picture of his home.

Unternehmen

compagnie

company

empresa

公司

What company do you work for?

Hacke

houe

hoe

azada

锄头

Use a hoe in the garden.

Boot   bateau

boat

barco   船

The boat is sailing.

frisch   frais

fresh

fresco   新鲜

All the fruit is fresh.

Bauernhof   ferme

farm

granja   农场

The farm has lots of animals.

Stühle   chaises

chair

sillas   椅子

He is sitting on the chair.

Puppe   poupée

doll

muñeca   娃娃

She is hugging her doll.

Nase   nez

nose

nariz   鼻子

My nose is running.

griechisch — grec

Greek

griego — 希腊语

Have you ever had Greek food?

Säule — colonne

column

columna — 柱

Did you read the newspaper column?

Eichhörnchen — écureuil

squirrel

ardilla — 松鼠

The squirrel is on the tree.

Samen   la graine

seed

semilla   种子

We will plant the seeds.

Nacht   nuit

night

noche   晚

We sleep at night.

oben   haut

top

tapas   最佳

We like to play with tops.

Ding   chose

thing

cosa   事情

I am thinking of many things.

Auto   voiture

car

coche   汽车

My car is fast

Kirche   église

church

iglesia   教会

Did you go to church?

Morgen — matin

morning

mañana — 早上

I wake up in the morning.

Ring — bague

ring

anillo — 环

The bird is holding a ring.

Uhr — l'horloge

watch

reloj — 时钟

My watch is ticking.

He worked in the city.

We live in the same house.

My mother loves me.

He is taking some pictures.

He is a nice father.

Do you have any rope?

Sauerstoff

oxygène

oxygen

oxígeno

氧

What is the symbol for oxygen?

Ente

canard

duck

pato

鸭

The duck is swimming.

Familie

famille

family

familia

家庭

How big is your family?

Diagramm   graphique

chart

gráfico   图表

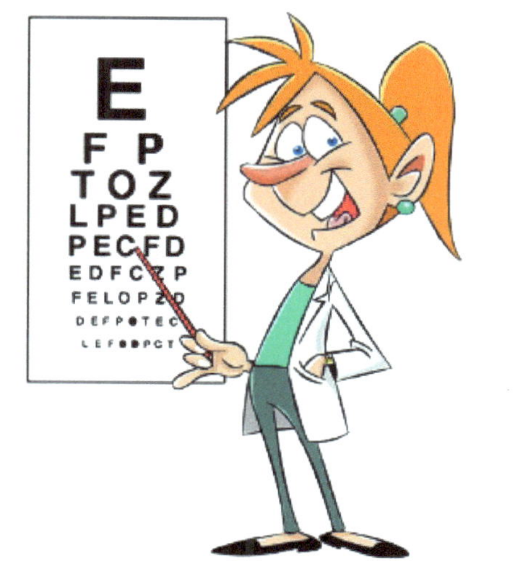

What does your medical chart say?

Fisch   poisson

fish

pez   鱼

There are two fish.

Tabelle   table

table

mesa   表

There is a toy on the table.

Ball

ball

balle

pelota

球

He is bouncing the ball.

Auge

eye

œil

ojo

眼睛

He is closing his eyes.

Rose

rose

rose

rosa

玫瑰

Thank you for the rose.

Gras   herbe

grass

césped   草

The goat is eating the grass.

Geld   argent

money

dinero   钱

I save money in my piggy bank.

Schwein   porc

pig

cerdo   猪

She is lying on the pig.

Straße — rue

street

calle — 街

They walk across the street.

Weg — façon

way

camino — 道路

They find a way back home.

Baby — bébé

baby

bebé — 宝宝

The baby is crawling.

The girls took a seat in the sand.

The bear is saying goodbye.

The cow is standing up.

Ei   oeuf

egg

huevo   蛋

The bunny has many eggs.

Junge   garçon

boy

chico   男孩

The boy is eating dinner.

Bedingungen   conditions

conditions

condiciones   条件

What are the weather conditions.

Männer

hommes

men

hombres

人

The men are arguing.

Gewehr

pistolet

gun

pistola

枪

We played with a water gun.

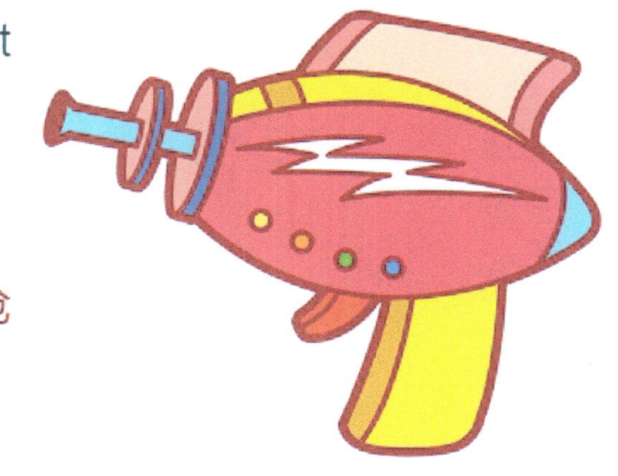

Pferd

cheval

horse

caballo

马

The horse is galloping.

letter

alphabet

字母

alfabeto

Learn English letters is fun.

Mais

blé

corn

maíz

玉米

I grow corn in the garden.

Blume

fleur

flower

flor

花

She is holding a flower.

Sonne

sun

soleil

dom

太阳

The sun is very bright.

Schnee

snow

neige

nieve

雪

I have fun in the snow.

Frankreich

France

france

francia

法国

Have you ever been to France?